TIME

FOR SOME

Good

NEWS

TIME

FOR SOME

Good

NEWS

IN TIMES OF UNCERTAINTY GOD HAS A PLAN
FOR YOU TO HAVE HOPE AND A FUTURE

EMMIE STANLEY

TIME FOR SOME GOOD NEWS
Copyright © 2024 by Emmie Stanley

Scripture marked (NKJV) taken from the New King James Version®. Copyright © 1982 by Thomas Nelson. Used by permission. All rights reserved. Scripture quotations marked (NLT) are taken from the Holy Bible, New Living Translation, copyright ©1996, 2004, 2015 by Tyndale House Foundation. Used by permission of Tyndale House Publishers, a Division of Tyndale House Ministries, Carol Stream, Illinois 60188. All rights reserved. Scripture quotations marked (NIV) are taken from the Holy Bible, New International Version®, NIV®. Copyright © 1973, 1978, 1984, 2011 by Biblica, Inc.™ Used by permission of Zondervan. All rights reserved worldwide. www.zondervan.comThe "NIV" and "New International Version" are trademarks registered in the United States Patent and Trademark Office by Biblica, Inc.™ Scripture quotations are from the ESV® Bible (The Holy Bible, English Standard Version®), © 2001 by Crossway, a publishing ministry of Good News Publishers. Used by permission. All rights reserved. The ESV text may not be quoted in any publication made available to the public by a Creative Commons license. The ESV may not be translated in whole or in part into any other language.

ISBN: 978-1-4866-2513-0
eBook ISBN: 978-1-4866-2514-7

Word Alive Press
119 De Baets Street Winnipeg, MB R2J 3R9
www.wordalivepress.ca

WORD ALIVE
—P R E S S—

Cataloguing in Publication information can be obtained from Library and Archives Canada.

I would like to dedicate this book to my four grandchildren: Riley, Lacey, Eve, and Elizebeth. Thank you, dear little ones, for giving me a reason to hold ground for a beautiful and hope-filled future. May you always know the peace that has been made available to you.

Love Grammy

Contents

Preface

The 60s and 70s in which I grew up were very turbulent years. The Vietnam War, the Cold War, and the Cuban missile crisis dominated news headlines. Even though I was just a child, I was quite aware of the world scene, since my dad was an avid news watcher and often talked about the seriousness of what was going on. It was hard for me to understand what everything meant and it made me feel anxious. I even wondered whether there was any hope for my future.

Now, at the current time in history, we are again confronted with crises and disasters that cause many to wonder about the future. Anxiety and mental health concerns are at all-time highs and we are definitely in need of some good news.

Just as the understanding in this little book transformed me from living pressed up against a wall of hopelessness to living a full, joyful, and meaningful life, may you also find in its pages the peace and brighter future your heart longs for.

Have you ever dreamed of a better life? Perhaps one where you wake up each morning feeling that your life has meaning, someone loves you, the world is at peace, and you never have to worry about money again?

Or maybe your dream is simple and more practical—you feel good, your mortgage is paid, and there is food on the table.

Whatever your hopes and dreams may be, one thing is certain: we all know in our heart of hearts that there must be more, something better, something that would fill the ache and longing inside us that never seems to be satisfied.

Fairy tales have a way of capturing our imagination and causing us to dream about what life could be. Take Cinderella, for example. Let's pretend for a moment that she was a real person. Imagine what her life might have been like, born into privilege, but, at the hand of her wicked stepmother, was cast down in rejection, cruelty, and even slavery. Hidden away in this dark world, it must have seemed to her like there was no hope.

But as the story goes, through unexpected circumstances she suddenly found herself in the palace of the prince, who fell in love with her, married her, and gave her hope and a bright new future.

You could say that Cinderella experienced a kind of salvation as she was removed from the harm, ruin, and loss that was her everyday life. When her new life began as the bride of the prince, her shame was removed, her hope was restored, and she experienced true love, joy, and freedom.

Cinderella didn't have to do anything to earn this beautiful new life. It was hers simply because the prince loved her. His love saw past her brokenness, shabby dress, shame, and soot-stained face. She only had to say yes.

Can fairy tales come true in real life? Is there a type of unconditional love—a salvation, if you will—that sees beyond our brokenness, forgives, heals our past, and delivers unto us a new life in which anything is possible?

The very word *salvation* includes within it the promise of safety, rescue, deliverance, health, victory, help, welfare, prosperity, and freedom. This is the kind of life most of us dream of and hope for. It's not a life in which everything is perfect and we will never know hardship again; rather, we can live with the confidence and expectation that we will overcome the obstacles before us and live with joy and hope in the midst of it all, all the while experiencing growing levels of peace and freedom.

Can I Feel Safe?

As a youth, I felt the world to be a very scary place. It was the Cold War. America had missiles pointed at Russia, Russia had missiles pointed at America, and many lived with the fear that someone might "push the button."

In our world today, most can relate to those same feelings. I was anxious and insecure, not knowing where to turn to find refuge from all the uncertainty. As a young adult, I found temporary escape through the party life, drinking, carousing, and fooling myself by pursuing meaningless relationships. Eventually the lustre of this lifestyle wore off and I was once again faced with a sense of hopelessness for what my future held.

One day while flipping through the TV channels, I came across a man talking about Jesus. I don't remember who he was or what he said, but I do remember thinking, *This guy has something I don't have, and I want it!*

So I did what he said and knelt at my coffee table. I asked Jesus to forgive me for the wrong things I had done and the bad choices I had made and invited Him to come into my life.

When I went to bed that night, I asked God, "Why don't you talk to me?" I had always heard that God did talk to people.

That very moment, I heard a voice in my head: "I am the way and the life!"

Okay, that was really weird, I thought.

But a little while later, when I started to actually read the Bible, I came across those very same words and knew that God had spoken to me. To me!

As time went on and I learned more about what God was really like, and how he really does have the whole world in his hands, I began to feel a peace I had never known before. I came to know what it means to feel safe and more hopeful for my future.

Every person is born with a deep need to know they are loved and safe. These continue to be core needs throughout our lives. We all ask ourselves, "Am I loved?" This question was answered by Jesus, who was willing to die to rescue us from the consequence of our sins, which were leading us to certain death. More about that a little later.

And what about the question, "Am I safe?" This isn't just about *feeling* safe, but actually *being* safe—in our homes, communities, and the bigger world, experiencing peace, security, and hope. Is that possible in this life?

Jesus offers us safety on two levels: in our here-and-now life and in our future-eternal life.

The Bible contains many promises, such as:

> He will not leave you nor forsake you. (Deuteronomy 31:6, NKJV)

> The angel of the Lord encamps all around those who fear Him, and delivers them. (Psalm 34:7, NKJV)

> Fear not, for I am with you; be not dismayed,
> for I am your God. I will strengthen you, yes, I
> will help you, I will uphold you with My righteous
> right hand. (Isaiah 41:10, NKJV)

Think about how Cinderella, had she been a real person, would have felt after moving out of her stepmother's house and into the palace with the prince. I think she would have experienced a new sense of value, love, and care. She would have finally felt safe, both physically and emotionally, and had hope for the future.

As I came into greater understanding of Jesus and what he did for me, I too experienced a growing degree of safety and hope.

Like Cinderella, we all have days when we feel like we need to be rescued. I'm reminded of a very old commercial featuring a woman who faced the common struggles of daily life. When she finally hit the breaking point, she put her hand to her forehead and loudly declared, "Oh Calgon, take me away!" She then proceeded to have her Calgon bubble bath… and her whole world became right again.

Oh that life could be that simple!

Well, some of us only face these daily challenges. For others, the situation is much more serious—such as marriage problems, health issues, housing insecurity, addictions, or a whole myriad of other difficulties.

Jesus offers us rescue, but rescue from what? The Bible says it this way: *"For he has rescued us from the dominion of darkness and brought us into the kingdom of the Son he loves…"* (Colossians 1:13–14, NIV)

When we invite Jesus into our lives, we are spiritually moved from a place of darkness into the kingdom of Jesus and his love!

Simply put, there are two kingdoms: the domain of darkness and the kingdom of light. These are the only two. There is no neutral place; we are either in one or the other.

One day, my husband and I went to the heart of downtown Vancouver for a night out. This was during the time when I was just starting to ponder life and God in a more serious way. I was teetering between living in darkness and seeking the light.

As I looked around the downtown scene, I had a surreal moment in which the homelessness, drunkenness, and general perversion all around me seemed to be highlighted in a supernatural way, as if God was showing me how real the darkness was. This was a life-changing moment for me.

The Bible says that the domain of darkness is ruled by an evil being known as Satan, whereas the kingdom of light is ruled by God (Father, Son, and Holy Spirit). Those who live in the domain of darkness typically don't encounter the love of God. They tend to live their lives with a perspective that says, "This is my life and I will live it as I please."

People who have given their lives to the kingdom of light have discovered that there is a real God who loves them and has good plans for their lives. What is their perspective? They tend to believe, "God's way works, and as I live by his principals I experience peace, hope, and wellness in every area."

Those who have chosen to enter the kingdom of God are called "redeemed." What does this mean? Think of it like when a person is kidnapped and a ransom is paid to get them back. This is what Jesus did when he died on the cross. He gave his life as a ransom for our lives. That's how much God loves and values every single person.

Here's another example. It's also like going to court to pay a fine, but you're unable to pay and consequently will be sent to prison. Even though you're guilty and deserve the penalty, the judge gets down from the bench, takes off his robes, and goes to the court clerk to pay your fine on your behalf. You are now free! It's a gift, no strings attached.

We have all been guilty of living our lives apart from honouring God. Like the judge, Jesus came down from heaven to die on the cross, to pay our debt so we can be free. This is God the Father's love and forgiveness for us, through his Son Jesus.

You must choose whether to receive this gift, but to be clear, it's a decision you need to make one way or the other.

The Bible says, *"For the wages of sin is death, but the gift of God is eternal life in Christ Jesus our Lord"* (Romans 6:23, NIV).

Why are the wages of sin death? Is it because God is punishing us? In fact, sin—which can simply be defined as "missing the mark"—has its own built-in consequences. Poor choices lead to poor outcomes which naturally lead toward both spiritual and physical death.

Poor choices are often the result of a lack of knowledge and determining to live according to our own way, whether or not it's in our best interest. When we operate without true knowledge and live in our own self-determination, we experience the kingdom of darkness and the result of sin, which is separation from God. God is life itself, the very source of life; hence sin, which cuts us off from God, also cuts us off from life.

As the Son of God, Jesus's life has more value than all human life put together. Since he himself did not sin, and never broke relationship with God, his life was more than enough to make up for every sin of every person who has ever lived. In this way, he paid the wages of all our sins on our behalf.

God is a good God who loves us and wants us to experience a good life. When we choose Jesus and move into his kingdom, we desire to please him. Although we're still human and will at times sin, his forgiveness continues to be available to us. We are secure in him.

Jesus's death on the cross has paid for our all of our sins once and for all time. The result is a turnaround in our lives, along with healing and the grace to overcome. We can experience peace even faced with the consequences of our own sin. When we align ourselves with his knowledge, as taught in the Bible, and start doing things his way, we experience new life, finally knowing what it means to be in the kingdom of light. The wages of our sin, death, have been paid for and we are freed to choose to do things his way, receiving his promise of a better life here and now and eternal life in heaven with him.

It is not God's heart or desire to send anyone to hell. However, we choose it for ourselves when we don't acknowledge and receive the gift of eternal life through what Jesus did for us.

He is the God who rescues us, translating us from the domain of darkness to the kingdom of his love! We were made to have a relationship with him. It is a free gift, and it is our choice.

You know that thing you struggle with? That thing you just can't seem to shake yourself loose from, no matter how many times you try? It could be a habit, such as smoking, eating too much, or some other kind of addiction. Perhaps you even harm yourself in some way. You've tried everything you can think of and are left wondering, *Why can't I overcome this?*

Remember that we are dealing with two kingdoms, one of darkness and one of light. The kingdom of darkness represents sickness, depression, loneliness, hopelessness, defeat... you get the picture. The kingdom of light, on the other hand, offers such benefits as hope, peace, joy, love, help, rescue, and health, to name a few!

These two kingdoms each operate in two realms: the natural realm (the world we can touch, see, taste, hear, and smell) and the spiritual realm (the unseen world, which is still real). The spiritual realm includes where God and the angels live, but it also includes the domain of darkness where the devil and his demons live.

The Bible tells us that God has eternally existed. We can't even comprehend that.

Angels, however, were created by God. Their main purposes are to worship him and help us. However, like people, angels have God given free will. This means they can think for themselves and make their own choices.

At the beginning, there were three senior angels who worked very closely with God. One of them was Lucifer, whose name meant "light bringer" (Isaiah 14:12–14). But a time came when Lucifer thought he was so important that *he* should be God. He led a coup against God in heaven, the outcome of which was that he and one-third of the angels who rebelled against God were cast out of heaven and sent down to the earth (Revelation 12:2–4).

Lucifer's name was changed to Satan, who is our adversary, the devil. The other rebellious angels, now referred to as demons, now live in the spiritual realm here on the earth, and their intent is to promote evil and darkness.

At many points in my life, I felt like something was trying to draw me against my will to the very things I was trying not to do. I often heard voices in my head telling me that I wasn't good enough, that nobody liked me, that I was too *this* or *that*, causing me to feel lonely and defeated. I wondered, *Why am I thinking like this?*

In time, I came to understand that these weren't just my own thoughts. Rather, these were the voices of evil entities. The work of the darkness is to steal, kill, and destroy. This is how it works; they can't make you do anything, but they can harass you until you believe it, and then act on it.

The Bible explains it this way:

> For we do not wrestle against flesh and blood, but against the rulers, against the authorities, against the cosmic powers over this present

> darkness, against the spiritual forces of evil in the
> heavenly places. (Ephesians 6:12, ESV)

Your seeming inability to overcome a challenge in your life may actually be worsened by the domain of darkness harassing you. Darkness tries very hard to remain secret and undercover, but now you know what you're fighting against. Knowledge is power, and knowing your enemy is the first step in being set free from what you struggle with.

When we cross over into the kingdom of light by giving our lives to Jesus, we become a new creation. The Bible refers to this as being born again. It's a fresh start.

> Therefore, if anyone is in Christ, he is a new cre-
> ation. The old has passed away; behold, the new
> has come. (2 Corinthians 5:17, ESV)

However, even though we have a fresh start, we still bring with us elements of our past, like habits, thought patterns, and attitudes. Some of these are good and others are typically unhelpful. As new creations learning what it means to live with Jesus, we begin a lifelong process of leaving behind our old ways of thinking and learning to think, act, and live as part of the kingdom of light.

When I invited Jesus into my life, one vice that I remember being set free from very quickly was swearing. For a girl, I had it pretty bad. Obviously I knew better, but something inside me found great satisfaction in running my rebellious mouth.

I grew up on a ranch and spoke like a cowboy; I was one of them. When I was ten years old, one of the boys in school told the teacher I had a swearing problem. Yes, it started that early!

However, when you have Jesus in your life you also have a natural desire to please him. It didn't take long to change once I made the decision to live for him —and with his help, it wasn't even hard to eradicate swearing from my life.

The Bible is literally a manual for life. Romans 12:2 tells us that we are to renew our minds. We do this by reading from scripture and learning how to practically apply it.

For example, when I was having health issues, I looked up the principles for healing and good health. As I learned how to think differently and apply my new understanding, my health improved dramatically. I will share more about this in the next section.

As we learn God's ways, we leave our old ways behind and get better results. This is part of the process of repentance, which simply means to turn and go the other way.

By applying these new principles, we work out our salvation. We embrace a lifestyle of growth and change. The result is that we are set free from our old problems and experience healthier, happier lives as we grow and walk in the truth.

> And you shall know the truth, and the truth shall make you free. (John 8:32, NKJV)

The more truth we know, the more we recognize the difference between God's voice, which speaks love and encouragement to us, and the voices of darkness that try to sabotage us. As we follow, grow in, and live in truth, we are delivered from those things that have hindered us, free from the voices that have harassed us, and are able to step forward in life, experiencing greater peace, freedom, and victory.

> When the righteous cry for help, the Lord hears
> and delivers them out of all their troubles. (Psalm
> 34:17, ESV)

Is Being Healthy Too Much to Hope For?

For most of my life, I struggled with underlying health issues. It was nothing major. In fact, it's hard to call it a "sickness." It was just a nagging weakness, similar to having allergies. But it undermined my strength and hindered me from doing all that I wanted to do, all that I should have been capable of doing.

As you read the stories of Jesus in the Bible, one of the most notable facts you'll probably notice is that he healed a lot of people. In fact, the Bible clearly states that his death on the cross wasn't intended only to pay for our sins, but also for our ability to live healed, healthy lives (1 Peter 2:24). This too is part of what it means to accept his gift of salvation.

I came to a point where I was ready to take a stand and believe that God wanted me to be well. I had occasionally experienced healing miracles in my life. For example, one day on the ranch I was chased by a steer and fell against a fence and cracked some of my ribs. I was in pain for days, so uncomfortable that I could hardly breathe. Then I asked someone to pray for me! Although my back was still very painful that afternoon, by the evening all the pain had gone. It was pretty amazing!

This new healing journey, however, was going to be a little different. It wasn't going to be instantaneous. In fact, it would be the most intense and profitable year of my entire life.

Through what Jesus did on the cross, God has made a multitude of promises. It's up to us to grow in our understanding and apply these promises to our own lives, proving them true as they become our new reality.

I spent a lot of time reading what the Bible says about health and healing. I also journaled and prayed for understanding. The more I learned, the more my expectation grew. I came to believe that I could be healed, that I could be stronger and have a greater capacity for life. This is what it looked like to work out my salvation. The promise was already available to me, but I had to learn how it worked and apply it to my situation.

I learned so much through this process that I came to see it was actually *better* than a miracle. It's kind of like the saying, "Give a man a fish and he will eat for a day, but teach him how to fish and he will eat for a lifetime." I grew in my understanding of God, faith, and how life works when I brought him and his ways into the picture. I also became more aware of the dark forces that harass me through fear and anxiety and cause me to focus more on sickness than God's heart for me to be healthy.

The Bible says, *"For as [a man] thinks in his heart, so is he"* (Proverbs 23:7, NKJV). We tend to experience the things we focus on. I had to learn to think on the truth and what God says instead of listening to those lying voices that undermined my quality of life.

It took about a year, but it really was one of the best years of my life. Since then, I have had a greater capacity for undertaking daily life. I feel stronger, have more energy, and live in much better health. This doesn't mean that I never get sick, but it's more of an occasional experience rather than an ongoing way of life. The fears and habits at the root of my problem were revealed and removed; my wrong thinking was replaced by the truth. Oh happy day!

Is It Okay to Be Rich?

It would likely be true to say that most of us have dreamed of being rich at some point in our lives. But what does it really mean to be rich? It is said that money cannot buy happiness, and that is essentially true.

How does the Bible define prosperity? It means experiencing wellness in every area of life. When we thrive emotionally and in our relationships, health, finances, and especially in our relationship with the God who loves us, we experience a truly rich and prosperous life.

> Beloved, I pray that you may prosper in all things
> and be in health, just as your soul prospers. (3
> John 2, NKJV)

Your soul encompasses your mind, will, and emotions. There is a connection between how healthy we are emotionally and spiritually (our prospering soul) and how we experience resulting prosperity (wellness) in all other areas of our lives.

A healthy, happy, well-balanced person is on track to live a prosperous life to a greater degree than one who is sick, bitter, depressed, and angry. So you could say that a prospering soul is one who has experienced healing, which leads to wellness in every area, potentially even resulting in success in every endeavour.

I'm sure it comes as no surprise to learn that true prosperity goes far beyond money. However, the Bible does talk a lot about money and its proper place in our lives. Money in itself isn't the root of all evil, but it's true that the *love* of money leads to evil.

It seems that God doesn't have a problem with us owning and enjoying the finer things of life, as heavens streets are paved with gold and its walls are decorated with beautiful gemstones of every description. And the Bible tells the stories of many men of God who were very rich, including Job, Abraham, Isaac, Jacob, David, and Solomon.

So what is the right perspective for us to hold about our finances? What is God the Father's heart for us on this important subject?

Deuteronomy 8:18 tells us that God gives us the ability to produce wealth. He wants us to be financially healthy. He is the provider of everything we need, from the very breath we breathe to the gifts, talents, creative ideas, and strength he gives us. We cannot achieve anything without him as our source.

God's system for life is summed up this way: you reap what you sow. It's like a farmer planting seed in his field. How you treat others, how you share your resources, and what you can expect to receive in return is directly related to what you're willing to invest.

In Luke 6:38, we are told,

> Give, and it will be given to you: good measure, pressed down, shaken together, and running over will be put into your bosom. For with the

> same measure that you use, it will be measured
> back to you. (NKJV)

God is a giver! He gave the ultimate gift of life: his Son Jesus. He highly values giving. And when we give—whether of our finances, time, or resources—God says that he will give back to us more than we gave away.

Simply said, you cannot outgive God. Giving, when done with the right motive—which involves truly caring for others—is an investment in your future, creating a healthy, joyful, and prosperous life that reflects his love and goodness.

True prosperity is wellness in every area of life, and this is part of the salvation promises Jesus died to make available to you.

Victory

When I was in my early twenties, I once heard someone say that I was born to win. That certainly was never my expectation or experience in life. It seemed to me like some people were just born with an ability to succeed in all they did; for others, life seemed to be a constant struggle—at best, it was hit and miss. My life felt like the latter.

This begs some questions. Is success random, or do we have some level of control over it? Are we born lucky? Does luck really have anything to do with our outcomes? How does success relate to this salvation we've been talking about?

With Jesus in our lives, we have victory on two levels. The first relates to what we've already covered: we have been translated from the domain of darkness into the kingdom of Light. This is a victory we cannot earn for ourselves. It came by Jesus paying our ransom when he died on the cross on our behalf. Through that act, we were set free from the grip of darkness on our lives.

This is a victory over death itself! Jesus is life, and with him in our lives death no longer has any hold on us. We will still die in the physical sense, but we have eternal life within us and have been promised to live with Jesus forever in heaven.

The truly freeing aspect of this is how totally free it is. It cannot be earned. We can't be good enough to deserve it. Once we have received the gift of eternal life, simply by acknowledging that our sin has separated us from God, it becomes our permanent condition. We receive his forgiveness and say yes to Jesus coming into our lives.

This is truly a victory over death, an attainment of the promise that we will have eternal life with him!

The second level of victory we experience as Christians is something we can realize as we walk out our day-to-day lives. Psalms 65:11 tells us, *"You crown the year with Your goodness, and Your paths drip with abundance"* (NKJV). The paths here refer to God's ways as laid out in the Bible.

In the Bible, we find instruction for success in every area of our lives, including health, relationships, business, government, marriage, child-rearing, finances, and so much more.

Think about it this way: the God who made us and loves us gave us a whole book telling us who he is, what he has done, and how we can live our best lives. As previously mentioned, it's a literal manual for life.

I have a tendency to tinker with new devices and try to figure out how they work without looking at the instructions. Normally this isn't very productive and I just end up frustrated, telling myself I should have just read the manual in the first place.

In the same way, we can tinker with our lives and try to get it right, or we can find out how life is meant to work by allowing the one who made us to personally teach us through the manual we have been given.

We are told in 2 Corinthians 2:14 that God always leads us in victory. The very fact that he leads us implies that we must follow.

The more we take time to read the Bible and listen to God speaking to us through it, following his lead and applying his principles, we will experience growing and ongoing victories.

In Jesus, we really have been born to win!

Liberty

It is possible to live in real freedom! Freedom from fear, anxiety, guilt, shame, addictions, lies, and our past. We can have the satisfaction of knowing the answer to the big questions of life. Why am I here? Am I loved? Where will I go after this life?

You can enjoy the freedom of being the person you were made to be, and live courageously while knowing that you are fulfilling the very purpose for which you were born. You can possess the joy and peace that can only be found in the truth of all that Jesus's love means for you, through a relationship with him.

Within this concept of salvation, and all that Jesus has done on our behalf, we can be rescued from the domain of darkness and come into the kingdom of light. God really does have the whole world in his hands, and as we look to him we can know that we are safe, because he is in control. We can overcome habits, addictions, and the harassing voices that rob us of our peace, holding us back from living the full life that God planned for us and wants us to enjoy.

The more we come to know this God who loves us and died for us, applying his principles to our lives, the more we will experience physical, mental, and emotional healing, which leads to a truly prosperous life. This is true freedom!

Free Will and Your Right to Choose

> Today I have given you the choice between life and death, between blessings and curses. Now I call on heaven and earth to witness the choice you make. Oh, that you would choose life, so that you and your descendants might live! You can make this choice by loving the Lord your God, obeying him, and committing yourself firmly to him. This is the key to your life. And if you love and obey the Lord, you will live long in the land… (Deuteronomy 30:19, NLT)

God has given you life, and what you do with it is your choice. However, his invitation and desire for you is to surrender that same life back to him, giving yourself over to his plan for you and fulfilling the purpose for which you are alive on the earth today.

> If you cling to your life, you will lose it; but if you give up your life for me, you will find it. (Matthew 10:39, NLT)

I hope that today you will choose life, to surrender to him and experience his salvation for you!

The following is a prayer you can pray to start your new life in Jesus:

> Dear Jesus, thank you for dying to pay for my sins, ransoming me from the domain of darkness. Forgive me for choosing to live separate from you and your way. I surrender my life and my plans to you now and ask you to fill me with your Spirit, enabling me to live for you, and with you, every day.

If you have said yes to Jesus today and agreed to surrender your life to his plans for you, you have just started on the most wonderful adventure and relationship of your life.

I encourage you to learn about your new life through reading the Bible and join a local church that will help you to understand what it means to be a child of God.

> "For I know the plans I have for you," declares the Lord, "plans to prosper you and not to harm you, plans to give you hope and a future." (Jeramiah 29:11, NIV)

About the Author

Emmie has worked in ministry for more than thirty years, including seventeen years on staff with Power to Change Canada, where she received training and experience in leadership and evangelism.

As director of the Power to Change Prayer ministry, Emmie led teams across Canada with a particular focus on praying for schools, as well as cities. She has also led evangelism and outreach teams focusing on the marginalized and homeless of her own city of Langley, British Columbia. Her unique opportunities to share the good news, particularly in the inner city, have come through serving meals, presenting the Alpha program, and offering spa services such as free manicures and haircuts.

Emmie has been privileged to enjoy hands-on ministry as well as teach and inspire others through workshops, retreats, and conferences. Currently Emmie leads the women's ministry at her local church.

Emmie can be reached at stanleyemmie370z@gmail.com.